AAT

Qualifications and Credit Framework (QCF)

LEVEL 3 DIPLOMA IN ACCOUNTING

QUESTION BANK

Accounts Preparation II

2011 Edition

First edition July 2010
Second edition July 2011

ISBN 9780 7517 9760 2

(Previous edition 9780 7517 8598 2)

British Library Cataloguing-in-Publication Data
A catalogue record for this book is available from the British
Library

Published by

BPP Learning Media Ltd
BPP House
Aldine Place
London W12 8AA

www.bpp.com/learningmedia

Printed in the United Kingdom

CONTENTS

A NOTE ABOUT COPYRIGHT

INTRODUCTION

This is BPP Learning Media's AAT Question Bank for Accounts Preparation II. It is part of a suite of ground breaking resources produced by BPP Learning Media for the AAT's assessments under the qualification and credit framework (QCF).

The Accounts Preparation II assessment will be **computer assessed**. As well as being available in the traditional paper format, this **Question Bank is available in an online format** where all questions and assessments are presented in a **style which mimics the style of the AAT's assessments.** BPP Learning Media believe that the best way to practise for an online assessment is in an online environment. However, if you are unable to practise in the online environment you will find that all tasks in the paper question bank have been written in a style that is as close as possible to the style that you will be presented with in your online assessment.

This Question Bank has been written in conjunction with the BPP Text, and has been carefully designed to enable students to practise all of the learning outcomes and assessment criteria for the units that make up Accounts Preparation II. It is fully up to date as at July 2011 and reflects both the AAT's Guidance and the specimen assessment provided by the AAT.

This Question Bank contains these key features:

- Tasks corresponding to each chapter of the Text. Some tasks are designed for learning purposes, others are of assessment standard

- The AAT's specimen assessment and answers for Accounts Preparation II

- Three further practice assessments

The emphasis in all tasks and assessments is on the practical application of the skills acquired.

VAT

You will find tasks throughout this question bank which need you to calculate or be aware of a rate of VAT. This is stated at 20% in these examples and questions.

If you have any comments about this book, please e-mail suedexter@bpp.com or write to Sue Dexter, Publishing Director, BPP Learning Media Ltd, BPP House, Aldine Place, London W12 8AA.

Question bank

Chapter 1

Task 1.1

Indicate whether each of the following balances is an asset, a liability, income, an expense or capital.

Balance	Asset ✓	Liability ✓	Income ✓	Expense ✓	Capital ✓
Salaries					
Bank overdraft					
Office costs					
Bank loan					
Capital					
Receivables (debtors)					
Purchases					
Discount received					

Task 1.2

Given below is a trial balance for a business. Indicate with a tick as to whether each item in the trial balance falls into the category of asset, liability, income, expense or capital.

Balance	Debit	Credit	Asset ✓	Liability ✓	Income ✓	Expense ✓	Capital ✓
	£	£					
Rent cost	11,400						
Sales		143,000					
Opening inventory (stock)	2,400						
Payables (creditors)		6,000					
Purchases	86,200						
Drawings	17,910						
Telephone costs	1,250						
Discounts received		80					
Distribution costs	400						
Motor vehicles	32,600						
Receivables (debtors)	11,900						
Discounts allowed	120						
Capital		40,000					
Wages	20,600						
Heat and light	1,600						
Computer	2,400						
Bank	300						
	189,080	189,080					

Task 1.3

A business has made sales during the year of £867,450. The opening inventory (stock) of goods was £24,578 and the closing inventory was £30,574. During the year there were purchases made of £426,489. Distribution costs for the year were £104,366 and administration expenses totalled £87,689.

What are the gross and net profit for the year?

Gross profit	£	
Net profit	£	

Task 1.4

What are the main categories of items that appear on a statement of financial position (balance sheet) for a business?

Task 1.5

Decide whether each of the following balances would be an asset or liability on the statement of financial position (balance sheet), or an item of income or expense in an income statement (profit and loss account). For the statement of financial position items indicate what types of asset or liability they are.

Balance	Asset ✓	Liability ✓	Income ✓	Expense ✓	Type of asset/liability
A company car					
Interest on a bank overdraft					
A bank loan repayable in five years					
Petty cash of £25					
The portion of rent paid covering the period after the statement of financial position date					
Freehold property					
Payment of wages for a manager with a two year service contract					
An irrecoverable (bad) debt written off					

Task 1.6

Describe the form and function of the statement of financial position (balance sheet) and the income statement (profit and loss account).

Statement of financial position (SFP)

Income Statement (IS)

Task 1.7

Computer software, although for long-term use in the business, is charged to the income statement (profit and loss account) when purchased as its value is small in comparison with the hardware.

Which accounting concept determines this treatment?

Task 1.8

Explain each of the following four objectives which determine an organisation's choice of accounting policies.

Relevance

Reliability

Comparability

Ease of understanding

Task 1.9

Classify the following items as long-term assets ('non-current (fixed) assets'), short-term assets ('current assets') or liabilities.

Classification	Non-current (fixed) assets ✓	Current assets ✓	Liabilities ✓
A PC used in the accounts department of a shop			
A PC on sale in an office equipment shop			
Wages due to be paid to staff at the end of the week			
A van for sale in a motor dealer's showroom			
A delivery van used in a grocer's business			
An amount owing to a bank for a loan for the acquisition of a van, to be repaid over 9 months			

Task 1.10

Fill in the missing words:

The trading account shows the ⬚ profit for the period

The income statement (profit and loss account) shows the ⬚ profit for the period.

Task 1.11

	Yes ✓	No ✓
Is a bank overdraft a current liability?		

Task 1.12

Which of the following is **not** an accounting concept

✓	
	Prudence
	Consistency
	Depreciation
	Accruals

Chapter 2

Task 2.1

A sole trader had a capital balance of £32,569 on 1 May 20X8. During the year ended 30 April 20X9 the business made a net profit of £67,458 and the owner withdrew cash totalling £35,480 and goods with a cost of £1,680.

What is the capital balance at 30 April 20X9?

£ [   ]

Task 2.2

A sole trader took goods from his business with a cost of £560 for his own personal use. What is the double entry for this transaction?

Debit	
Credit	

Task 2.3

The draft trial balance for a sole trader for the year ended 30 June is as follows:

	£
Machinery at cost	140,000
Motor vehicles at cost	68,000
Furniture and fittings at cost	23,000
Accumulated depreciation – machinery	64,500
Accumulated depreciation – motor vehicles	31,200
Accumulated depreciation – furniture and fittings	13,400

The depreciation charges for the year to 30 June have not yet been accounted for and the sole trader's depreciation policies are:

Machinery	20% on cost
Motor vehicles	35% reducing balance
Furniture and fittings	20% reducing balance

What is the total carrying amount (net book value) of the non-current (fixed) assets that will appear in the statement of financial position (balance sheet) at 30 June?

£ [   ]

Task 2.4

A sole trader has produced the following final trial balance:

Trial balance at 31 May 20X8

	Debit	Credit
	£	£
Bank		1,650
Capital		74,000
Payables (creditors)		40,800
Receivables (debtors)	60,000	
Discounts allowed	2,950	
Discounts received		2,000
Drawings	30,000	
Furniture and fittings at cost	24,500	
Electricity	2,950	
Insurance	2,300	
Miscellaneous expenses	1,500	
Motor expenses	3,100	
Motor vehicles at cost	48,000	
Purchases	245,000	
Allowance for receivables		1,200
Accumulated depreciation – furniture and fittings		8,550
– motor vehicles		29,800
Rent	3,400	
Sales		369,000
Opening inventory (stock)	41,000	
Telephone costs	1,950	
VAT		4,100
Wages	52,000	
Closing inventory	43,500	43,500
Depreciation expense – furniture and fittings	2,450	
Depreciation expense – motor vehicles	7,800	
Irrecoverable (bad) debts expense	1,700	
Accruals		1,000
Prepayments	1,500	
	575,600	575,600

Prepare the financial statements for the year ended 31 May 20X8.

Income statement (profit and loss account) for the year ended 31 May 20X8

	£	£
Sales		
Cost of goods sold		
Gross profit		
Total expenses		
Net profit		

Statement of financial position (balance sheet) as at 31 May 20X8

	Cost	Depreciation	Carrying amount (net book value)
	£	£	£
Non-current (fixed) assets			
Current assets			
Current liabilities			
Net current assets			
Net assets			
Financed by:			

Task 2.5

Given below is the final trial balance of a sole trader for his year ended 30 June 20X8.

Final trial balance as at 30 June 20X8

	£	£
Administration expenses	7,490	
Bank	2,940	
Capital		60,000
Payables (creditors)		20,200
Receivables (debtors)	14,000	
Discounts allowed	2,510	
Discounts received		2,550
Distribution costs	1,530	
Drawings	14,600	
Machinery at cost	58,400	
Motor vehicles at cost	22,100	
Office costs	1,570	
Purchases	121,200	
Allowance for receivables		280
Accumulated depreciation		
– Machinery		35,040
– Motor vehicles		12,785
Sales		167,400
Inventory (stock) at 1 July 20X7	15,400	
Selling expenses	6,140	
VAT		3,690
Wages	16,700	
Inventory at 30 June 20X8	18,200	18,200
Irrecoverable debts expense	2,820	
Accruals		680
Prepayments	440	
Depreciation expense – machinery	11,680	
Depreciation expense – motor vehicles	3,105	
	320,825	320,825

Prepare the financial statements of the sole trader for the year ended 30 June 20X8.

Income statement (profit and loss account) for the year ended 30 June 20X8

	£	£
Sales		
Cost of goods sold		
Gross profit		
Total expenses		
Net profit		

Statement of financial position (balance sheet) as at 30 June 20X8

	Cost	Depreciation	Carrying amount (net book value)
	£	£	£
Non-current (fixed) assets			
Current assets			
Current liabilities			
Net current assets			
Net assets			
Financed by:			

Task 2.6

A sole trader has prepared his financial statements from his trial balance. Extracts from that trial balance are given below:

	£	£
Sales		184,321
Purchases	91,201	
General expenses	16,422	

You are required to prepare journal entries showing how these accounts would be closed off at the year end.

	Debit	Credit
	£	£

Task 2.7

A trial balance contains the following balances:

	£
Opening inventory (stock)	2,000
Closing inventory	4,000
Purchases	20,000
Purchases returns	400
Settlement discounts received	1,600

What is the cost of sales?

£

Task 2.8

For a statement of financial position (balance sheet) to balance, which of the following statements is wrong?

✓	
	Net assets = owner's funds
	Net assets = capital + profit + drawings
	Net assets = capital + profit - drawings
	Non-current (fixed) assets + net current assets = capital + profit - drawings

Chapter 3

Task 3.1

On 1 January 20X8, a business had assets of £10,000 and liabilities of £7,000. By 31 December 20X8 it had assets of £15,000 and liabilities of £10,000. The owner had contributed capital of £4,000. Use the T account below to calculate how much profit or loss had the business made over the year.

£ [   ]

Capital account

£	£

Task 3.2

The net assets of a business totalled £14,689 at 1 January 20X8 and £19,509 at 31 December 20X8. The owner did not pay any additional capital into the business but did withdraw £9,670 in drawings.

Use the T account below to calculate the profit or loss made by the business in the year.

£ [   ]

Capital account

£	£

Task 3.3

A business has net assets of £31,240 on 31 May 20X8. On 1 June 20X7 the net assets of the business were £26,450. The owner knows that he took £12,300 of drawings out of the business during the year in cash and £560 of goods for his own use.

Use the T account below to calculate the profit or loss made by the business in the year.

£ [   ]

Capital account

£	£

Task 3.4

A business had net assets at the start of the year of £23,695 and at the end of the year of £28,575. The business made a profit of £17,370 for the year.

Use the T account below to calculate the drawings made by the owner in the year.

£ [   ]

Capital account

£	£

Task 3.5

The owner of a small shop provides you with the following information about its transactions for the month of May 20X8:

	£
Till rolls showing amounts paid into till	5,430
Paying in slip stub showing amount paid into bank from till	4,820
Cheques to payables (creditors) totalling	3,980

The till always has a £100 cash float and the balance on the bank account at 1 May was £368 and at 30 May was £414. The owner has taken cash drawings out of the till and out of the bank account directly.

Use the T accounts below to calculate the drawings made by the owner in the month.

£ [   ]

Cash account

£		£

Bank account

£		£

Task 3.6

A small shop keeps a cash float of £250 in the till. The bank statement for the month of March 20X9 shows that the amount of cash paid into the bank for the month was £7,236. The owner keeps a record of the amounts of cash paid directly out of the till and knows that these consisted of wages of £320, cleaning costs of £50 and drawings of £1,050.

Use the T account below to calculate the sales in the month.

£ [   ]

Cash account

£		£

Task 3.7

A business has a balance on its receivables (debtors) account of £1,589 at the start of October 20X8 and this has risen to £2,021 by the end of October. The paying in slips for the month show that £5,056 was received from receivables during the month and discounts of £127 were allowed.

Use the T account below to calculate the credit sales in the month.

£ [   ]

Receivables account

£		£

Task 3.8

The balance on a business's payables (creditors) account at 1 March 20X9 was £4,266 and by 31 March was £5,111. During the month cheques paid to payables totalled £24,589 and discounts received were £491.

Use the T account below to calculate the credit purchases in the month.

£ [   ]

Payables account

£		£

Task 3.9

A shop operates with a mark-up on cost of 20%. The purchases for the month of May totalled £3,600 and the inventory (stock) at the start of May was £640 and at the end of May was £570.

What were the sales for the month?

£ [   ]

Task 3.10

A shop operates with a mark-up on cost of 30%. The sales for the period were £5,200 and the stock (inventory) at the start and end of the period were £300 and £500.

What were the purchases for the period?

£ [   ]

Task 3.11

A shop operates on the basis of a profit margin of 20%. The purchases for the month of April totalled £5,010 and the stock (inventory) at the start and the end of the month was £670 and £980 respectively.

What are the sales for the period?

£ [   ]

Task 3.12

Sheena Gordon has been trading for just over 12 months as a dressmaker. She has kept no accounting records at all, and she is worried that she may need professional help to sort out her financial position, and she has approached you.

You meet with Sheena Gordon and discuss the information that you require her to give you. Sometime later, you receive a letter from Sheena Gordon providing you with the information that you requested, as follows:

(i)   She started her business on 1 October 20X7. She opened a business bank account and paid in £5,000 of her savings.

(ii)   During October she bought the equipment and the inventory (stock) of materials that she needed. The equipment cost £4,000 and the inventory of materials cost £1,800. All of this was paid for out of the business bank account.

(iii)   A summary of the business bank account for the twelve months ended 30 September 20X8 showed the following.

	£		£
Capital	5,000	Equipment	4,000
Cash banked	27,000	Opening inventory of materials	1,800
		Purchases of materials	18,450
		General expenses	870
		Drawings	6,200
		Balance c/d	680
	32,000		32,000

(iv) All of the sales are on a cash basis. Some of the cash is paid into the bank account while the rest is used for cash expenses. She has no idea what the total value of her sales is for the year, but she knows that she has spent £3,800 on materials and £490 on general expenses. She took the rest of the cash not banked for her private drawings. She also keeps a cash float of £100.

(v) The gross profit margin on all sales is 50%.

(vi) She estimates that all the equipment should last for five years. You therefore agree to depreciate it using the straight-line method.

(vii) On 30 September 20X8, the payables (creditors) for materials amounted to £1,400.

(viii) She estimates that the cost of inventory (stock) of materials that she had left at the end of the year was £2,200.

You are required to:

    (a) Calculate the total purchases for the year ended 30 September 20X8.

      £ [   ]

    (b) Calculate the total cost of sales for the year ended 30 September 20X8.

      £ [   ]

    (c) Calculate the sales for the year ended 30 September 20X8.

      £ [   ]

    (d) Show the entries that would appear in Sheena Gordon's cash account.

Cash account

£		£

    (e) Calculate the total drawings made by Sheena Gordon throughout the year.

      £ [   ]

    (f) Calculate the figure for net profit for the year ended 30 September 20X8.

      £ [   ]

Task 3.13

(a) At 1 January 20X1 suppliers were owed £10,000, by 31 December 20X1 they were owed £8,000. In the year, receivables (debtors) and payables (creditors) contras were £3,500, and £350 of debit balances were transferred to receivables. Credit purchases were £60,000 and £2,500 of discounts were received.

What was paid to suppliers during the year?

	✓
£55,650	
£56,000	
£56,350	
£58,000	

(b) A business has opening inventory (stock) of £30,000 and achieves a mark-up of 25% on cost. Sales totalled £1,000,000, purchases were £840,000. Calculate closing inventory.

	✓
£30,000	
£40,000	
£120,000	
£70,000	

Task 3.14

A sole trader has net assets of £19,000 at 30 April 20X9. During the year to 30 April 20X9 he introduced £9,800 additional capital into the business. Profits were £8,000, of which he withdrew £4,200. His capital at 1 May 20X8 was

✓	
	£3,000
	£5,400
	£13,000
	£16,600

Chapter 4

Task 4.1

Jim, Rob and Fiona are in partnership sharing profits in the ratio of 4 : 3 : 2. At 1 January 20X8 the balances on their current accounts were:

Jim   £2,000

Rob   £1,000 (debit)

Fiona   £3,500

During the year to 31 December 20X8 the partnership made a net profit of £135,000 and the partners' drawings during the year were:

Jim   £58,000

Rob   £40,000

Fiona   £32,000

Write up the partners' current accounts for the year ended 31 December 20X8.

Current account – Jim

£		£

Current account – Rob

£		£

Current account – Fiona

	£		£
	————		————
	════		════

....

Task 4.2

Josh and Ken are in partnership sharing profits in a ratio of 2 : 1. Ken is allowed a salary of £8,000 per annum and both partners receive interest on their capital balances at 3% per annum. An extract from their trial balance at 30 June 20X8 is given below.

		£
Capital	Josh	40,000
	Ken	25,000
Drawings	Josh	21,000
	Ken	17,400
Current account (credit balances)	Josh	1,300
	Ken	800

The partnership made a net profit for the year ended 30 June 20X8 of £39,950.

Write up the profit appropriation account and the partners' current accounts and show the balances that would appear in the statement of financial position (balance sheet) for the capital accounts and current accounts.

Profit appropriation account

	£		£

Current account – Josh

	£			£

Current account – Ken

	£			£

Statement of financial position balances

....

Task 4.3

Jo, Emily and Karen are in partnership sharing profits equally. Emily is allowed a salary of £4,000 per annum and all partners receive interest on their capital balances at 5% per annum.

Given below is the final trial balance of the partnership between Jo, Emily and Karen at 30 June 20X8.

Final trial balance

	Debit £	Credit £
Advertising	3,140	
Bank	1,400	
Capital Jo		25,000
Emily		15,000
Karen		10,000
Payables (creditors)		33,100
Current accounts Jo		1,000
Emily		540
Karen		230
Receivables (debtors)	50,000	
Drawings Jo	12,000	
Emily	10,000	
Karen	10,000	
Electricity	4,260	
Furniture and fittings at cost	12,500	
Furniture and fittings – accumulated depreciation		7,025
Insurance	1,800	
Machinery at cost	38,000	
Machinery – accumulated depreciation		23,300
Allowance for receivables		1,500
Purchases	199,000	
Sales		306,000
Inventory (stock) at 1 July 20X7	23,400	
Sundry expenses	2,480	
Telephone expenses	2,150	
VAT		1,910
Wages	43,200	
Inventory (stock) at 30 June 20X8	24,100	24,100
Depreciation expense – machinery	7,600	
Depreciation expense – furniture and fittings	1,825	
Irrecoverable (bad) debts expense	1,550	
Accruals		400
Prepayments	700	
	449,105	449,105

You are required to:

(a) Prepare the income statement (profit and loss account) for the year ended 30 June 20X8

(b) Write up the profit appropriation account and partners' current accounts showing their share of profits and their drawings

(c) Prepare the statement of financial position (balance sheet) as at 30 June 20X8

(a) Income statement **(profit and loss account) for the year ended 30 June 20X8**

	£	£
Sales		
Cost of goods sold		
Gross profit		
Total expenses		
Net profit		

(b) **Appropriation of profit**

		£	£
Net profit			
Profit available for distribution			
Profit share			

Current account – Jo

	£		£

Current account – Emily

	£		£

Current account – Karen

	£		£

(c)   **Statement of financial position (balance sheet) as at 30 June 20X8**

	Cost	Depreciation	Carrying amount (net book value)
	£	£	£
Non-current (fixed) assets			
Current assets			
Current liabilities			
Net current assets			
Net assets			
Financed by:			

Task 4.4

Ian and Max have been in partnership for a number of years sharing profits in the ratio of 2 : 1. The net assets of the partnership total £145,000 and it is believed that in addition the partnership has goodwill of £18,000. Len is to be admitted to the partnership on 1 June 20X8 and is to pay in £32,600 of capital. After Len has been admitted the profits will be shared 2 : 2 : 1.

Write up the partners' capital accounts given below to reflect the goodwill adjustment and the admission of the new partner.

Capital accounts

	Ian £	Max £	Len £		Ian £	Max £	Len £
				Bal b/d	85,000	60,000	

Task 4.5

Theo, Deb and Fran have been in partnership for a number of years but on 31 December 20X8 Deb is to retire. The credit balances on the partners' capital and current accounts at that date are:

		£
Capital	Theo	84,000
	Deb	62,000
	Fran	37,000
Current	Theo	4,500
	Deb	1,300
	Fran	6,200

Before the retirement of Deb the partners had shared profits in the ratio of 3 : 2 : 1. However after Deb's retirement the profit sharing ratio between Theo and Fran is to be 2 : 1. The goodwill of the partnership on 31 December 20X8 is estimated to be £54,000. The agreement with Deb is that she will be paid £10,000 at the date of retirement and the remainder of the amount that is due to her will take the form of a loan to the partnership.

Write up the partners' capital and current accounts to reflect Deb's retirement.

Capital accounts

	Theo £	Deb £	Fran £		Theo £	Deb £	Fran £

Current accounts

	Theo £	Deb £	Fran £		Theo £	Deb £	Fran £

Task 4.6

During the year to 30 September 20X8 the partnership of Will and Clare Evans made a net profit of £90,000. From 1 October 20X7 until 30 June 20X8 the partnership agreement was as follows:

		Per annum
		£
Salaries	Will	10,000
	Clare	15,000
Interest on capital 3% of the opening capital balance		
Profit share	Will	two-thirds
	Clare	one-third

However on 1 July 20X8 the partnership agreement was changed as follows:

		£
Salaries	Will	12,000
	Clare	20,000

Interest on capital 3% of the opening capital balance

Profit share	Will	three-quarters
	Clare	one-quarter

The opening balances at 1 October 20X7 on their capital and current accounts were as follows:

		£
Capital	Will	80,000
	Clare	50,000
Current	Will	2,000 (credit)
	Clare	3,000 (debit)

During the year ended 30 September 20X8 Will made drawings of £44,000 and Clare made drawings of £37,000.

Prepare the partnership profit appropriation account and the partners' current accounts for the year ended 30 September 20X8.

Profit appropriation account

	1 October 20X7 to 30 June 20X8	1 July 20X8 to 30 Sept 20X8	Total
	£	£	£
Profit for distribution			
Profit share			

Current accounts

	Will £	Clare £		Will £	Clare £

Task 4.7

Mary Rose, Nelson Victory and Elizabeth Second are in partnership together hiring out river boats. Mary has decided to retire from the partnership at the end of the day on 31 March 20X9. You have been asked to finalise the partnership accounts for the year ended 31 March 20X9 and to make the entries necessary to account for the retirement of Mary from the partnership on that day.

You have been given the following information:

(1)   The profit for the year ended 31 March 20X9 was £106,120.

(2)   The partners are entitled to the following salaries per annum.

	£
Mary	18,000
Nelson	16,000
Elizabeth	13,000

(3)   Interest on capital is to be paid at a rate of 12% on the balance at the beginning of the year on the capital accounts. No interest is paid on the current accounts.

(4)   Cash drawings in the year amounted to:

	£
Mary	38,000
Nelson	30,000
Elizabeth	29,000

(5)   The balances on the current and capital accounts at 1 April 20X8 were as follows.

	Capital accounts		Current accounts
	£		£
Mary	28,000 (credit)	Mary	£2,500 (credit)
Nelson	26,000 (credit)	Nelson	£2,160 (credit)
Elizabeth	22,000 (credit)	Elizabeth	£1,870 (credit)

(6)   The profit-sharing ratios in the partnership are currently:

Mary	4/10
Nelson	3/10
Elizabeth	3/10

On the retirement of Mary, Nelson will put a further £40,000 of capital into the business. The new profit-sharing ratios will be:

Nelson	6/10
Elizabeth	4/10

(7)   The goodwill in the partnership is to be valued at £90,000 on 31 March 20X9. No separate account for goodwill is to be maintained in the books of the partnership. Any adjusting entries in respect of goodwill are to be made in the capital accounts of the partners.

(8)   Any amounts to the credit of Mary on the date of her retirement should be transferred to a loan account.

You are required to:

(a)   Prepare the partners' capital accounts as at 31 March 20X9 showing the adjustments that need to be made on the retirement of Mary from the partnership

(b)   Prepare an appropriation account for the partnership for the year ended 31 March 20X9

(c)   Prepare the partners' current accounts for the year ended 31 March 20X9

(d)   Show the balance on Mary's loan account as at 31 March 20X9

(a)   **Partners' capital accounts**

Partners' capital accounts

	Mary £	Nelson £	Elizabeth £		Mary £	Nelson £	Elizabeth £

(b)   **Mary, Nelson and Elizabeth**

Profit appropriation account for the year ended 31 March 20X9

	£	£
Net profit		106,120
Net profit available for distribution		
Profit share		

(c)

Partners' current accounts

	Mary £	Nelson £	Elizabeth £		Mary £	Nelson £	Elizabeth £

(d)

Mary: loan account

	£		£

Task 4.8

Fill in the missing word regarding the definition of a partnership.

A partnership is a relationship between persons carrying on a business in common with a view to

---

Task 4.9

What is the double entry for drawings made by a partner?

Debit	
Credit	

Task 4.10

What is the double entry to record interest earned on partners' capital account balances?

✓		
	Debit	partners' current accounts
	Credit	profit and loss appropriation account
	Debit	profit and loss appropriation account
	Credit	partners' current accounts
	Debit	profit and loss appropriation account
	Credit	cash
	Debit	profit and loss appropriation account
	Credit	partners' capital account

Answer bank

Answer bank

Chapter 1

Task 1.1

Balance	Asset ✓	Liability ✓	Income ✓	Expense ✓	Capital ✓
Salaries				✓	
Bank overdraft		✓			
Office costs				✓	
Bank loan		✓			
Capital					✓
Receivables (debtors)	✓				
Purchases				✓	
Discount received			✓		

Task 1.2

Trial balance	Debit	Credit	Asset ✓	Liability ✓	Income ✓	Expense ✓	Capital ✓
	£	£					
Rent cost	11,400					✓	
Sales		143,000			✓		
Opening inventory (stock)	2,400					✓	
Payables (creditors)		6,000		✓			
Purchases	86,200					✓	
Drawings	17,910						✓
Telephone costs	1,250					✓	
Discounts received		80			✓		
Distribution costs	400					✓	
Motor vehicles	32,600		✓				
Receivables (debtors)	11,900		✓				
Discounts allowed	120					✓	
Capital		40,000					✓
Wages	20,600					✓	
Heat and light	1,600					✓	
Computer	2,400		✓				
Bank	300		✓				
	189,080	189,080					

Task 1.3

Gross profit	£	446,957
Net profit	£	254,902

Workings

	£	£
Sales		867,450
Cost of sales:		
Opening inventory (stock)	24,578	
Purchases	426,489	
	451,067	
Less: closing inventory	(30,574)	
		(420,493)
Gross profit		446,957
Distribution costs		(104,366)
Administration costs		(87,689)
Net profit		254,902

....

Task 1.4

- Non-current (fixed) assets
- Current assets – inventories (stocks), receivables (debtors), bank and cash
- Current liabilities – payables (creditors)
- Long term liabilities – loans
- Capital
- Net profit
- Drawings

....

Task 1.5

Balance	Asset ✓	Liability ✓	Income ✓	Expense ✓	Type of asset/liability
A company car	✓				Non-current (fixed) asset
Interest on a bank overdraft				✓	
A bank loan repayable in five years		✓			Long-term liability
Petty cash of £25	✓				Current asset
The portion of rent paid covering the period after the statement of financial position date	✓				Prepayment (current asset)
Freehold property	✓				Non-current asset
Payment of wages for a manager with a two year service contract				✓	
An irrecoverable (bad) debt written off				✓	

Task 1.6

Statement of financial position (SFP)

A statement of financial position (SFP) is a list of the assets, liabilities and capital of a business at a given moment. Assets are divided into non-current (fixed) assets and current assets. Liabilities may be current or non-current (long term).

Income Statement (IS)

An income statement (IS) matches the revenue earned in a period with the costs incurred in earning it. It is usual to distinguish between a gross profit (sales revenue less the cost of goods sold) and a net profit (being the gross profit less the expenses of selling, distribution, administration and so on).

Task 1.7

> Materiality

Task 1.8

> **Relevance**
>
> Financial information is said to be relevant if it has the ability to influence the economic decisions of the users of that information and is provided in time to influence those decisions. Where an organisation faces a choice of accounting policies they should choose the one that is more relevant in the context of the final accounts as a whole. Materiality also affects relevance.

> **Reliability**
>
> In the financial statements:
>
> * The figures should represent the substance of the transactions or events
>
> * The figures should be free from bias, or neutral
>
> * The figures should be free from material errors
>
> * A degree of caution should have been applied in making judgements where there is uncertainty

> **Comparability**
>
> Information in financial statements is used by many different people and organisations. It is much more useful to these users if it is comparable over time and also with similar information about other businesses. The selection of appropriate accounting policies and their consistent use should provide such comparability.

> **Ease of understanding**
>
> Accounting policies should be chosen to ensure ease of understanding for users of financial statements. For this purpose users are assumed to have a reasonable knowledge of business and economic activities and accounting and a willingness to study the information diligently.

Task 1.9

Classification	Non-current (fixed) assets ✓	Current assets ✓	Liabilities ✓
A PC used in the accounts department of a shop	✓		
A PC on sale in an office equipment shop		✓	
Wages due to be paid to staff at the end of the week			✓
A van for sale in a motor dealer's showroom		✓	
A delivery van used in a grocer's business	✓		
An amount owing to a bank for a loan for the acquisition of a van, to be repaid over 9 months			✓

Task 1.10

The trading account shows the | gross | profit for the period.

The income statement (profit and loss account) shows the | net | profit for the period.

Task 1.11

	Yes ✓	No ✓
Is a bank overdraft a current liability?	✓	

Task 1.12

Which of the following is **not** an accounting concept

✓	
	Prudence
	consistency
	Depreciation
✓	Accruals

Chapter 2

Task 2.1

£	62,867

Workings

	£
Opening capital	32,569
Net profit for the year	67,458
	100,027
Less: drawings (35,480 + 1,680)	37,160
Closing capital	62,867

Task 2.2

Debit	Drawings
Credit	Purchases

Task 2.3

£	79,100

Workings

Depreciation charges

– machinery	=	£140,000 x 20%	=	£28,000
– motor vehicles	=	(£68,000 – 31,200) x 35%	=	£12,880
– furniture and fittings	=	(£23,000 – 13,400) x 20%	=	£1,920

	Cost	Accumulated depreciation	Carrying amount (net book value)
	£	£	£
Machinery	140,000	92,500	47,500
Motor vehicles	68,000	44,080	23,920
Furniture and fittings	23,000	15,320	7,680
			79,100

Task 2.4

Income statement (profit and loss account) for the year ended 31 May 20X8

		£	£
Sales			369,000
Less:	Cost of sales		
	Opening inventory (stock)	41,000	
	Purchases	245,000	
		286,000	
	Less: closing inventory	(43,500)	
Cost of goods sold			242,500
Gross profit			126,500
Less:	Expenses		
	Discounts allowed	2,950	
	Electricity	2,950	
	Discounts received	(2,000)	
	Insurance	2,300	
	Miscellaneous expenses	1,500	
	Motor expenses	3,100	
	Rent	3,400	
	Telephone costs	1,950	
	Wages	52,000	
	Depreciation furniture and fittings	2,450	
	motor vehicles	7,800	
	Irrecoverable (bad) debts	1,700	
Total expenses			80,100
Net profit			46,400

Statement of financial position (balance sheet) as at 31 May 20X8

	Cost £	Depreciation £	Carrying amount (net book value) £
Non-current (fixed) assets			
Furniture and fittings	24,500	8,550	15,950
Motor vehicles	48,000	29,800	18,200
	72,500	38,350	34,150
Current assets			
Inventory (stock)		43,500	
Receivables (debtors)	60,000		
Less: allowance	1,200		
		58,800	
Prepayments		1,500	
		103,800	
Current liabilities			
Payables (creditors)	40,800		
Bank overdraft	1,650		
Accruals	1,000		
VAT	4,100		
		47,550	
Net current assets			56,250
Net assets			90,400
Financed by:			
Opening capital			74,000
Net profit			46,400
			120,400
Less: drawings			30,000
			90,400

....

Task 2.5

Income statement (profit and loss account) for the year ended 30 June 20X8

		£	£
Sales			167,400
Less:	Cost of sales		
	Opening inventory (stock)	15,400	
	Purchases	121,200	
		136,600	
Less:	closing inventory	(18,200)	
Cost of goods sold			(118,400)
Gross profit			49,000
Less:	Expenses		
	Administration expenses	7,490	
	Distribution costs	1,530	
	Discounts allowed	2,510	
	Discounts received	(2,550)	
	Office costs	1,570	
	Selling expenses	6,140	
	Wages	16,700	
	Irrecoverable (bad) debts	2,820	
	Depreciation expense:		
	machinery	11,680	
	motor vehicles	3,105	
Total expenses			(50,995)
Net loss			(1,995)

Statement of financial position (balance sheet) as at 30 June 20X8

	Cost	Depreciation	Carrying amount (net book value)
	£	£	£
Non-current (fixed) assets			
Machinery	58,400	35,040	23,360
Motor vehicles	22,100	12,785	9,315
	80,500	47,825	32,675
Current assets			
Inventory (stock)		18,200	
Receivables (debtors)	14,000		
Less: allowance	(280)		
		13,720	
Prepayments		440	
Bank		2,940	
		35,300	
Current liabilities			
Payables (creditors)	20,200		
Accruals	680		
VAT	3,690		
		24,570	
Net current assets			10,730
Net assets			43,405
Financed by:			
Capital			60,000
Net loss for the year			(1,995)
			58,005
Less: drawings			(14,600)
			43,405

Task 2.6

	Debit	Credit
	£	£
Sales	184,321	
Income statement (profit and loss) ledger account		184,321
Income statement (profit and loss) ledger account	91,201	
Purchases		91,201
Income statement (profit and loss) ledger account	16,422	
General expenses		16,422

Task 2.7

£ | 17,600

Workings

	£
Purchases	20,000
Less: purchases returns	(400)
	19,600
Add: opening inventory (stock)	2,000
Less: closing inventory	(4,000)
Cost of sales	17,600

Task 2.8

✓	
	Net assets = owner's funds
✓	Net assets = capital + profit + drawings
	Net assets = capital + profit - drawings
	Non-current (fixed) assets + net current assets = capital + profit – drawings

Drawings reduce capital, so they must be deducted.

Chapter 3

Task 3.1

£	2,000 loss

Workings

	£
Assets 1 January 20X8	10,000
Liabilities 1 January 20X8	7,000
Owner's capital at 1 January 20X8	3,000
	£
Assets 31 December 20X8	15,000
Liabilities 31 December 20X8	10,000
Owner's capital at 31 December 20X8	5,000

Capital account

	£		£
Drawings	0	Balance b/d	3,000
Loss (bal fig)	2,000		
Balance c/d	5,000	Capital introduced	4,000
	7,000		7,000

Task 3.2

£	14,490 profit

Workings

Capital account

	£		£
Drawings	9,670	Balance b/d	14,689
Balance c/d	19,509	Profit (bal fig)	14,490
	29,179		29,179

Task 3.3

£ | 17,650 profit

Workings

Capital account

	£		£
Drawings	12,860	Balance b/d	26,450
Balance c/d	31,240	Profit (bal fig)	17,650
	44,100		44,100

Task 3.4

£ | 12,490

Workings

Capital account

	£		£
Drawings (bal fig)	12,490	Balance b/d	23,695
Balance c/d	28,575	Profit	17,370
	41,065		41,065

Task 3.5

£ | 1,404 |

Workings

Cash account

	£		£
Balance b/d	100	Bankings	4,820
Sales	5,430	Drawings (bal fig)	610
		Balance c/d	100
	5,530		5,530

Bank account

	£		£
Balance b/d	368	Payables (creditors)	3,980
Bankings	4,820	Drawings (bal fig)	794
		Balance c/d	414
	5,188		5,188

Total drawings	£
Cash	610
Bank	794
	1,404

Task 3.6

£ | 8,656

Workings

Cash account

	£		£
Balance b/d	250	Bankings	7,236
Sales (bal fig)	8,656	Wages	320
		Cleaning costs	50
		Drawings	1,050
		Balance c/d	250
	8,906		8,906

Task 3.7

£ | 5,615

Workings

Receivables (debtors) account

	£		£
Balance b/d	1,589	Bank	5,056
Sales (bal fig)	5,615	Discount allowed	127
		Balance c/d	2,021
	7,204		7,204

Task 3.8

£ | 25,925

Workings

Payables (creditors) account

	£		£
Bank	24,589	Balance b/d	4,266
Discounts received	491	Purchases (bal fig)	25,925
Balance c/d	5,111		
	30,191		30,191

Task 3.9

£ | 4,404 |

Workings

	£	%
Sales (bal fig)	4,404	120
Cost of sales (640 + 3,600 – 570)	3,670	100
Gross profit	734	20

· ·

Task 3.10

£ | 4,200 |

Workings

	£	£	%
Sales		5,200	130
Cost of sales			
Opening inventory (stock)	300		
Purchases (bal fig)	4,200		
	4,500		
Less: closing inventory	(500)		
Cost of sales (5,200 x 100/130)		4,000	100
Gross profit		1,200	30

· ·

Task 3.11

£ | 5,875 |

Workings

	£	%
Sales (bal fig)	5,875	100
Cost of sales (670 + 5,010 – 980)	4,700	80
Gross profit	1,175	20

· ·

Task 3.12

(a)

	£
Opening inventory (stock)	1,800
Payments: bank	18,450
cash	3,800
Payables (creditors)	1,400
Total purchases	25,450

(b)

	£
Purchases (from (a))	25,450
Closing inventory (stock)	(2,200)
Total cost of sales	23,250

(c)

	£
Cost of sales (from (b))	23,250
Total sales (x 2) (gross profit margin 50%)	46,500

(d)

Cash account

	£		£
Sales (from (c))	46,500	Bank account	27,000
		Materials	3,800
		General expenses	490
		Drawings (balancing figure)	15,110
		Bal c/d (float)	100
	46,500		46,500

(e)

	£
Bank account	6,200
Cash account (from (d))	15,110
Total drawings	21,310

(f)

	£	£
Sales (from (c))		46,500
Cost of sales (from (b))		(23,250)
Gross profit		23,250
General expenses (870 + 490)	1,360	
Depreciation (4,000/5)	800	
		(2,160)
Net profit		21,090

Task 3.13

(a)

£55,650	
£56,000	
£56,350	✓
£58,000	

Workings

Payables (creditors) control account

	£		£
Contra	3,500	Balance b/d	10,000
Discounts received	2,500	Transfers to receivables (debtors)	350
Cash paid (bal fig)	56,350	Purchases	60,000
Balance c/d	8,000		
	70,350		70,350

(b)

£30,000	
£40,000	
£120,000	
£70,000	✓

Workings

	£	%
Sales	1,000,000	125
Cost of sales	800,000	100
Opening inventory (stock)	30,000	
Purchases	840,000	
	870,000	
Closing inventory (bal fig)	(70,000)	
Cost of sales	800,000	

Task 3.14

✓	
	£3,000
✓	£5,400
	£13,000
	£16,600

Working

	£
Opening capital (balancing figure)	5,400
Capital introduced	9,800
Profits	8,000
	23,200
Drawings	(4,200)
Net assets	19,000

Chapter 4

Task 4.1

Current account – Jim

	£		£
Drawings	58,000	Balance b/d	2,000
Balance c/d	4,000	Profit share (135,000 × 4/9)	60,000
	62,000		62,000
		Balance b/d	4,000

Current account – Rob

	£		£
Balance b/d	1,000	Profit share (135,000 × 3/9)	45,000
Drawings	40,000		
Balance c/d	4,000		
	45,000		45,000
		Balance b/d	4,000

Current account – Fiona

	£		£
Drawings	32,000	Balance b/d	3,500
Balance c/d	1,500	Profit share (135,000 × 2/9)	30,000
	33,500		33,500
		Balance b/d	1,500

Task 4.2

Profit appropriation account

	£		£
Salary – Ken	8,000	Net profit b/d	39,950
Interest			
Josh (40,000 × 3%)	1,200		
Ken (25,000 × 3%)	750		
Balance c/d	30,000		
	39,950		39,950
		Profit for distribution	30,000
Profit share			
Josh (30,000 × 2/3)	20,000		
Ken (30,000 × 1/3)	10,000		
	30,000		30,000

Current account – Josh

	£		£
Drawings	21,000	Balance b/d	1,300
Balance c/d	1,500	Profit share (1,200 + 20,000)	21,200
	22,500		22,500
		Balance b/d	1,500

Current account – Ken

	£		£
Drawings	17,400	Balance b/d	800
		Profit share	
Balance c/d	2,150	(8,000 + 750 + 10,000)	18,750
	19,550		19,550
		Balance b/d	2,150

Statement of financial position (balance sheet) balances	
Capital accounts:	
- Josh	£40,000
- Ken	£25,000
Current accounts:	
- Josh	£1,500
- Ken	£2,150

Task 4.3

(a) **Income statement (profit and loss account) for the year ended 30 June 20X8**

			£	£
Sales				306,000
Less:	Cost of sales			
	Opening inventory (stock)		23,400	
	Purchases		199,000	
			222,400	
Less: closing inventory			24,100	
Cost of good sold				198,300
Gross profit				107,700
Less:	Expenses			
	Advertising		3,140	
	Electricity		4,260	
	Insurance		1,800	
	Sundry expenses		2,480	
	Telephone expenses		2,150	
	Wages		43,200	
	Depreciation	machinery	7,600	
		furniture and fittings	1,825	
Irrecoverable (bad) debts			1,550	
Total expenses				68,005
Net profit				39,695

(b) **Appropriation of profit**

	£	£
Net profit		39,695
Salary – Emily		(4,000)
Interest Jo (25,000 x 5%)		(1,250)
Emily (15,000 x 5%)		(750)
Karen (10,000 x 5%)		(500)
Profit available for distribution		33,195
Profit share (33,195/3)		
Jo		11,065
Emily		11,065
Karen		11,065
		33,195

Current account – Jo

	£		£
Drawings	12,000	Bal b/d	1,000
Bal c/d	1,315	Interest	1,250
		Profit	11,065
	13,315		13,315
		Bal b/d	1,315

Current account – Emily

	£		£
Drawings	10,000	Bal b/d	540
Bal c/d	6,355	Salary	4,000
		Interest	750
		Profit	11,065
	16,355		16,355
		Bal b/d	6,355

Current account – Karen

	£		£
Drawings	10,000	Bal b/d	230
Bal c/d	1,795	Interest	500
		Profit	11,065
	11,795		11,795
		Bal b/d	1,795

(c)   **Statement of financial position (balance sheet) as at 30 June 20X8**

	Cost	Accumulated depreciation	Carrying amount (net book value)
	£	£	£
Non-current (fixed) assets			
Machinery	38,000	23,300	14,700
Furniture and fittings	12,500	7,025	5,475
	50,500	30,325	20,175
Current assets			
Inventory (stock)		24,100	
Receivables (debtors)	50,000		
Less: allowance	1,500		
		48,500	
Prepayments		700	
Bank		1,400	
		74,700	
Current liabilities			
Payables (creditors)	33,100		
Accruals	400		
VAT	1,910		
		35,410	
Net current assets			39,290
Net assets			59,465
Financed by:			
Capital accounts	Jo		25,000
	Emily		15,000
	Karen		10,000
			50,000
Current accounts	Jo	1,315	
	Emily	6,355	
	Karen	1,795	
			9,465
			59,465

Task 4.4

Capital accounts

	Ian £	Max £	Len £		Ian £	Max £	Len £
				Bal b/d	85,000	60,000	
Goodwill	7,200	7,200	3,600	Goodwill	12,000	6,000	
Balance c/d	89,800	58,800	29,000	Bank			32,600
	97,000	66,000	32,600		97,000	66,000	32,600

Task 4.5

Capital accounts

	Theo £	Deb £	Fran £		Theo £	Deb £	Fran £
				Balance b/d	84,000	62,000	37,000
				Current a/c		1,300	
Goodwill	36,000		18,000	Goodwill	27,000	18,000	9,000
Bank		10,000					
Loan		71,300					
Balance c/d	75,000		28,000				
	111,000	81,300	46,000		111,000	81,300	46,000

Current accounts

	Theo £	Deb £	Fran £		Theo £	Deb £	Fran £
Capital a/c		1,300		Balance b/d	4,500	1,300	6,200
Balance c/d	4,500		6,200				
	4,500	1,300	6,200		4,500	1,300	6,200

Task 4.6

Profit appropriation account

	1 October 20X7 to 30 June 20X8	1 July 20X8 to 30 Sept 20X8	Total
	£	£	£
Net profit 9/12 and 3/12 × £90,000	67,500	22,500	90,000
Salaries			
Will (9/12 × 10,000) and (3/12 × 12,000)	(7,500)	(3,000)	(10,500)
Clare (9/12 × 15,000) and (3/12 × 20,000)	(11,250)	(5,000)	(16,250)
Interest			
Will 9/12 and 3/12 × £2,400	(1,800)	(600)	(2,400)
Clare 9/12 and 3/12 × £1,500	(1,125)	(375)	(1,500)
Profit for distribution	45,825	13,525	59,350
Profit share			
Will (2/3 × 45,825) and (3/4 × 13,525)	30,550	10,144	40,694
Clare (1/3 × 45,825) and (1/4 × 13,525)	15,275	3,381	18,656
	45,825	13,525	59,350

Current accounts

	Will £	Clare £		Will £	Clare £
Balance b/d		3,000	Balance b/d	2,000	
Drawings	44,000	37,000	Salaries	10,500	16,250
Balance c/d	11,594		Interest	2,400	1,500
			Profit share	40,694	18,656
			Balance c/d		3,594
	55,594	40,000		55,594	40,000

Task 4.7

(a) **Partners' capital accounts**

Partners' capital accounts

	Mary £	Nelson £	Elizabeth £		Mary £	Nelson £	Elizabeth £
Goodwill (6:4)	–	54,000	36,000	Balance b/d	28,000	26,000	22,000
Loan				Cash		40,000	
(bal. fig)	69,860	–	–	Goodwill (4:3:3)	36,000	27,000	27,000
Balance c/d	–	39,000	13,000	Current a/c	5,860		
	69,860	93,000	49,000		69,860	93,000	49,000

(b) **Mary, Nelson and Elizabeth**

Profit appropriation account for the year ended 31 March 20X9

	£	£
Net profit		106,120
Less: partners' salaries		
Mary	18,000	
Nelson	16,000	
Elizabeth	13,000	
		47,000
Less: interest on capital		
Mary (£28,000 x 12%)	3,360	
Nelson (£26,000 x 12%)	3,120	
Elizabeth (£22,000 x 12%)	2,640	
		9,120
Net profit available for distribution		50,000
Profit share		
Mary 4/10		20,000
Nelson 3/10		15,000
Elizabeth 3/10		15,000
		50,000

(c)

Partners' current accounts

	Mary £	Nelson £	Elizabeth £		Mary £	Nelson £	Elizabeth £
Drawings	38,000	30,000	29,000	Balance b/d	2,500	2,160	1,870
Capital a/c	5,860	–	–	Interest on capital	3,360	3,120	2,640
Balance c/d	–	6,280	3,510	Salaries	18,000	16,000	13,000
				Profit	20,000	15,000	15,000
	43,860	36,280	32,510		43,860	36,280	32,510

(d)

Mary: loan account

	£		£
Balance c/d	69,860	Capital a/c	69,860
	69,860		69,860

Task 4.8

profit

Task 4.9

Debit

Current account

Credit

Bank or Purchases

Task 4.10

✓		
	Debit	partners' current accounts
	Credit	profit and loss appropriation account
✓	Debit	profit and loss appropriation account
	Credit	partners' current accounts
	Debit	profit and loss appropriation account
	Credit	cash
	Debit	profit and loss appropriation account
	Credit	partners' capital account

Interest on partners' capital is an appropriation of profit (debit appropriation account). Since partners have earned the money through their investment in the business, their current accounts should be credited with it.

SAMPLE ASSESSMENT
ACCOUNTS PREPARATION II

Time allowed: 2 hours

Section 1

Task 1.1

This task is about finding missing figures in ledger accounts where the records are incomplete.

You are working on the final accounts of a business for the year ended 31 March 20X1. You have the following information:

Day book summaries	Goods	VAT	Total
	£	£	£
Sales	134,000	26,800	160,800
Purchases	90,000	18,000	108,000

Balances as at	31 March X0	31 March X1
	£	£
Trade receivables (debtors)	15,700	14,300
Trade payables (creditors)	9,800	10,200

All sales and purchases are on credit terms.

Further information:	Net £	VAT £	Total £
Office expenses	3,600	720	4,320

Office expenses are not included in the purchases day book.

Bank summary	Dr £		Cr £
Balance b/d	9,620	Travel expenses	1,600
Trade receivables	158,320	Office expenses	4,230
Interest received	63	Trade payables	103,470
		HMRC for VAT	7,315
		Drawings	26,000
		Payroll expenses	11,090
		Balance c/d	14,298
	168,003		168,003

(a) Using the figures given above, prepare the payables (purchases) ledger control account for the year ended 31 March 20X1. Show clearly discounts as the balancing figure.

Payables ledger control account

	£		£

(b) Find the closing balance for VAT by preparing the VAT control account for the year ended 31 March 20X1. Use the figures given on the previous page.

Note: The business is not charged VAT on its travel expenses.

VAT control

	£		£
		Balance b/d	1,800

Task 1.2

This task is about calculating missing balances and the accounting equation.

You are given the following information about a sole trader as at 1 April 20X0:

The value of assets and liabilities were:

• Non-current (fixed) assets at net book value	£12,500
• Trade receivables (debtors)	£2,450
• Bank (overdrawn)	£860
• Trade payables (creditors)	£1,380

There were no other assets or liabilities.

(a) Calculate the capital account balance as at 1 April 20X0.

£

(b) On 30 April 20X0, a new computer is purchased on credit. Tick the boxes to show what effect this transaction will have on the balances. You must choose ONE answer for EACH line.

Balances	Debit ✓	Credit ✓	No change ✓
Non-current (fixed) assets			
Trade receivables (debtors)			
Trade payables (creditors)			
Bank			
Capital			

(c) Which of the following is best described as a current asset? Choose ONE answer.

	✓
An item of inventory (stock) that will be sold in the next month.	
A delivery van that will be sold in the next month.	
A loan that will be paid back to the bank in the next month.	
A purchase invoice for insurance that will be paid in the next month.	

Section 2

Task 2.1

This task is about preparing final accounts for sole traders.

You have the following trial balance for a sole trader known as Onyx Trading. All the necessary year-end adjustments have been made.

(a) Prepare an income statement (profit and loss account) for the business for the year ended 31 March 20X1.

Onyx Trading
Trial balance as at 31 March 20X1

	Dr £	Cr £
Accruals		1,500
Bank	1,660	
Capital		9,000
Closing inventory (stock)	17,000	17,000
Depreciation charge	5,100	
Discounts allowed	3,760	
Drawings	12,000	
General expenses	30,845	
Machinery at cost	20,400	
Machinery accumulated depreciation		10,200
Opening inventory	18,520	
Prepayments	2,000	
Purchases	110,740	
Payables (purchases) ledger control account		14,920
Rent	13,200	
Sales		209,890
Receivables (sales) ledger control account	18,145	
VAT		4,860
Wages	14,000	
	267,370	267,370

Onyx Trading
Income statement (profit and loss account) for the year ended 31 March 20X1

	£	£
Sales		
Cost of goods sold		
Gross profit		
Less:		
Total expenses		
Net profit		

(b) Indicate where the drawings should be shown in the final accounts. Choose ONE from:

	✓
As an addition to capital	
As a deduction from capital	
As an addition to expenses	
As a deduction from expenses	

(c) Identify ONE valid reason for producing a trial balance from:

	✓
It proves that no errors have been made.	
It provides a net profit figure.	
It shows where figures appear in the financial statements.	
It proves that double entry has taken place.	

Task 2.2

This task is about accounting for partnerships.

You have the following information about a partnership:

The partners are Sam and Terry.

- Riva was admitted to the partnership on 1 April 20X1 when she introduced £50,000 to the bank account.

- Profit share, effective until 31 March 20X1:

  - Sam   50%
  - Terry   50%

- Profit share, effective from 1 April 20X1:

  - Sam   40%
  - Terry   40%
  - Riva   20%

- Goodwill was valued at £36,000 on 31 March 20X1.

- Goodwill is to be introduced into the partners' capital accounts on 31 March and then eliminated on 1 April.

(a) Prepare the capital account for Riva, the new partner, showing clearly the balance carried down as at 1 April 20X1.

Capital account – Riva

	£		£
		Balance b/d	0

(b) Complete the following sentence by selecting the appropriate phrase from the picklist in each case:

When a partner retires from a partnership business, the balance on the [_____] must be transferred to the [_____].

Picklist:

business bank account
partner's capital account
partner's current account

Task 2.3

This task is about partnership accounts. (Note for students: the two parts of this task are independent of each other, and in the assessment you would be presented with only one of them.)

(a) You have the following information about a partnership business:

- The financial year ends on 31 March.

- The partners at the beginning of the year were Asma, Ben and Chris.

- Asma retired on 30 September 20X0.

- Partners' annual salaries:

    - Asma   £20,500
    - Ben   £25,000
    - Chris   nil

- Partners' interest on capital:

    - Asma   £1,500 per full year
    - Ben   £1,500 per full year
    - Chris   £1,500 per full year

- Profit share, effective until 30 September 20X0:

    - Asma   50%
    - Ben   25%
    - Chris   25%

- Profit share, effective from 1 October 20X0:

    - Ben   60%
    - Chris   40%

Net profit for the year ended 31 March 20X1 was £100,000. You can assume that profits accrued evenly during the year.

Prepare the appropriation account for the partnership for the year ended 31 March 20X1.

Partnership Appropriation account for the year ended 31 March 20X1

	1 April X0 – 30 September X0 £	1 October X0 – 31 March X1 £	Total £
Net profit			
Salaries:			
Asma			
Ben			
Chris			
Interest on capital:			
Asma			
Ben			
Chris			
Profit available for distribution			

Profit share			
Asma			
Ben			
Chris			
Total profit distributed			

(b) You have the following information about a partnership:

- The financial year ends on 31 March.

- The partners are Asma, Ben and Chris.

- Partners' annual salaries:

    - Asma   £8,250
    - Ben   £18,000
    - Chris   nil

- Partners' capital account balances as at 31 March 20X1:

    - Asma   £25,000
    - Ben   £50,000
    - Chris   £50,000

Interest on capital is charged at 3% per annum on the capital account balance at the end of the financial year.

- The partners share the remaining profit of £40,000 as follows:

    - Asma   20%
    - Ben   50%
    - Chris   30%

- Partners' drawings for the year:

    - Asma   £16,000
    - Ben   £40,000
    - Chris   £13,000

Prepare the current accounts for the partners for the year ended 31 March 20X1. Show clearly the balances carried down. You MUST enter zeros where appropriate in order to obtain full marks. Do NOT use brackets, minus signs or dashes.

Current accounts

	Asma £	Ben £	Chris £		Asma £	Ben £	Chris £
Balance b/d	400	0	0	Balance b/d	0	1,500	300

Task 2.4

Partnership statement of financial position (balance sheet)

This task is about preparing a partnership statement of financial position.

You are preparing the statement of financial position for the Onyx Partnership for the year ended 31 March 20X1. The partners are Jon and Pat.

All the necessary year-end adjustments have been made, except for the transfer of profit to the current accounts of the partners.

Before sharing profits the balances of the partners' current accounts are:

- Jon £250 credit
- Pat £356 credit

Each partner is entitled to £5,000 profit share.

(a) Calculate the balance of each partner's current account after sharing profits. Fill in the answers below.

Current account balance: Jon	£	
Current account balance: Pat	£	

Note: these balances will need to be transferred into the statement of financial position of the partnership which follows.

You have the following trial balance. All the necessary year-end adjustments have been made.

(b) Prepare a statement of financial position (balance sheet) for the partnership as at 31 March 20X1. You need to use the partners' current account balances that you have just calculated. Do NOT use brackets, minus signs or dashes.

Onyx Partnership
Trial balance as at 31 March 20X1

	Dr £	Cr £
Accruals		850
Administration expenses	38,890	
Bank	3,936	
Capital – Jon		30,000
Capital – Pat		25,000
Cash	350	
Closing inventory (stock)	22,570	22,570
Current account – Jon		250
Current account – Pat		356
Depreciation charge	4,185	
Disposal of non-current (fixed) asset	800	
Motor vehicles at cost	37,500	
Motor vehicles accumulated depreciation		16,125
Opening inventory	20,475	
Allowance for receivables		900
Change in allowance for receivables	85	
Purchases	85,724	
Payables (purchases) ledger control account		24,600
Sales		162,324
Receivables (sales) ledger control account	47,000	
Selling expenses	24,735	
VAT		3,275
Total	286,250	286,250

Onyx Partnership
Trial balance as at 31 March 20X1

	Cost £	Depreciation £	Carrying amount (net book value) £
Non-current (fixed) assets			
Current assets			
Current liabilities			
Net current assets			
Net assets			
Financed by:	Jon	Pat	Total

SAMPLE ASSESSMENT
ACCOUNTS PREPARATION II

ANSWERS

Section 1

Task 1.1

(a) Payables (purchases) ledger control account

	£		£
Bank	103,470	Balance b/d	9,800
Discounts received	4,130	Purchases day book	108,000
Balance c/d	10,200		
	117,800		117,800

(b) VAT control

	£		£
Purchases day book	18,000	Balance b/d	1,800
Office expenses	720	Sales day book	26,800
Bank	7,315		
Balance c/d	2,565		
	28,600		28,600

Task 1.2

(a) £12,710 (12,500 + 2,450 – 860 – 1,380)

(b)

	Debit ✓	Credit ✓	No change ✓
Non-current (fixed) assets	✓		
Trade receivables (debtors)			✓
Trade payables (creditors)		✓	
Bank			✓
Capital			✓

(c) An item of inventory (stock) that will be sold in the next month.

Section 2

Task 2.1

(a) **Onyx Trading**
Income statement (profit and loss account) for the year ended 31 March 20X1

	£	£
Sales		209,890
Opening inventory (stock)	18,520	
Purchases	110,740	
Closing inventory	(17,000)	
Cost of goods sold		112,260
Gross profit		97,630
Less:		
Depreciation charge	5,100	
Discounts allowed	3,760	
General expenses	30,845	
Rent	13,200	
Wages	14,000	
Total expenses		66,905
Net profit		30,725

(b) As a deduction from capital.

(c) It proves that double entry has taken place.

Task 2.2

(a) **Capital account – Riva**

	£		£
Goodwill	7,200	Balance b/d	0
Balance c/d	42,800	Bank	50,000
	50,000		50,000

(b) When a partner retires from a partnership business, the balance on the **partner's current account** must be transferred to the **partner's capital account**.

Task 2.3

(a) **Partnership appropriation account for the year ended 31 March 20X1**

	1 April X0 – 30 September X0 £	1 October X0 – 31 March X1 £	Total £
Net profit	50,000	50,000	100,000
Salaries:			
Asma	10,250	0	10,250
Ben	12,500	12,500	25,000
Chris	0	0	0
Interest on capital:			
Asma	750	0	750
Ben	750	750	1,500
Chris	750	750	1,500
Profit available for distribution	25,000	36,000	61,000

Profit share:			
Asma	12,500	0	12,500
Ben	6,250	21,600	27,850
Chris	6,250	14,400	20,650
Total profit distributed	25,000	36,000	61,000

(b) **Current accounts**

	Asma £	Ben £	Chris £		Asma £	Ben £	Chris £
Balance b/d	400	0	0	Balance b/d	0	1,500	300
Drawings	16,000	40,000	13,000	Salaries	8,250	18,000	0
Balance c/d	600	1,000	800	Interest on capital	750	1,500	1,500
				Profit share	8,000	20,000	12,000
	17,000	41,000	13,800		17,000	41,000	13,800

Task 2.4

(a) Jon

£5,250 (250 + 5,000)

Pat

£5,356 (356 + 5,000)

(b) **Onyx Partnership**
   Statement of financial position (balance sheet) as at 31 March 20X1

	Cost £	Depreciation £	Carrying amount (net book value) £
Non-current (fixed) assets			
Motor vehicles at cost	37,500	16,125	21,375
Current assets			
Inventory (stock)		22,570	
Trade receivables (debtors)		46,100	
Bank		3,936	
Cash		350	
		72,956	
Current liabilities			
Trade payables (creditors)	24,600		
VAT	3,275		
Accruals	850		
		28,725	
Net current assets			44,231
Net assets			65,606

Financed by:	Jon	Pat	Total
Capital accounts	30,000	25,000	55,000
Current accounts	5,250	5,356	10,606
	35,250	30,356	65,606

PRACTICE ASSESSMENT 1
ACCOUNTS PREPARATION II

Time allowed: 2 hours

Section 1

Task 1.1

This task is about finding missing figures in ledger accounts where the records are incomplete.

You are working on the final accounts of a business for the year ended 31 March 20X1. You have the following information:

Day book summaries	Goods	VAT	Total
	£	£	£
Sales	125,400	25,080	150,480
Purchases	76,000	15,200	91,200

Balances as at	31 March X0	31 March X1
	£	£
Trade receivables (debtors)	16,360	15,270
Trade payables (creditors)	13,280	12,950
Cash in till	300	250

You also find receipts in the cash till for cash purchases of £400.

Bank summary	Dr £		Cr £
Cash banked from till	2,900	Balance b/d	850
Trade receivables	142,650	Administration expenses	3,280
Interest received	520	Trade payables	92,330
		HMRC for VAT	6,820
		Drawings	2,900
		Payroll expenses	12,550
		Balance c/d	27,340
	146,070		146,070

(a) Using the figures given above, prepare the receivables (sales) ledger control account for the year ended 31 March 20X1. Show clearly discounts allowed as the balancing figure.

Receivables ledger control account

	£		£

(b) Find the figure for cash sales by preparing the cash in till account for the year ended 31 March 20X1. Use the figures given on the previous page.

Note: The business does not charge VAT on its cash sales.

Cash in till

	£		£

Task 1.2

This task is about calculating missing balances and the accounting equation.

You are given the following information about a sole trader as at 1 November 20XX:

The value of assets and liabilities were:

• Non-current (fixed) assets at net book value	£17,250
• Trade receivables (debtors)	£6,250
• Cash at bank	£1,280
• Capital	£21,000

There were no other assets or liabilities.

(a) Calculate the trade payables (creditors) account balance as at 1 November 20XX.

£

(b) On 30 April 20X0, cash is paid to a credit supplier, with some discount taken. Tick the boxes to show what effect this transaction will have on the balances. You must choose ONE answer for EACH line.

Balances	Debit ✓	Credit ✓	No change ✓
Income			
Trade receivables (debtors)			
Trade payables (creditors)			
Bank			
Expenses			

(c) Which TWO of the following are accurate representations of the accounting equation? Choose TWO answers.

	✓
Assets + Liabilities = Capital	
Assets – Liabilities = Capital	
Assets = Liabilities - Capital	
Assets = Liabilities + Capital	

Section 2 – Final accounts

Task 2.1

This task is about preparing financial statements for sole traders.

You have the following trial balance for a sole trader, Martha Tidfill. All the necessary year-end adjustments have been made.

(a) Prepare an income statement (profit and loss account) for the business for the year ended 31 August 20X4.

Martha Tidfill

Trial balance as at 31 August 20X4

	Dr £	Cr £
Accruals		1,250
Bank	2,190	
Capital		20,000
Closing inventory (stock)	15,200	15,200
Depreciation expense	4,750	
Discounts allowed	1,920	
Drawings	15,000	
Heat and light	11,620	
Motor vehicles accumulated depreciation		7,600
Motor vehicles at cost	25,400	
Office costs	27,690	
Opening inventory	17,690	
Prepayments	1,120	
Purchases	105,280	
Payables (purchases) ledger control account		18,280
Sales		199,560
Receivables (sales) ledger control account	17,960	
VAT		3,920
Wages	19,990	
	265,810	265,810

Martha Tidfill

Income statement (profit and loss account) for the year ended 31 August 20X4

	£	£
Sales		
Cost of goods sold		
Gross profit		
Total expenses		
Net profit		

(b) Indicate where the accruals balance should be shown in the financial statements. Choose ONE from:

	✓
Non-current (fixed) assets	
Current assets	
Current liabilities	
Non-current liabilities	

(c) When there are conditions of uncertainty, a degree of caution should be exercised when making judgements relating to the preparation of accounts. This is a description of the accounting principle of

	✓
Relevance	
Prudence	
Comparability	
Ease of understanding	

Task 2.2

This task is about accounting for partnerships.

You have the following information about a partnership:

The partners are Idris and Leonard.

- Patricia was admitted to the partnership on 1 January 20X3 when she introduced £25000 to the bank account.

- Profit share, effective until 31 December 20X2:

    - Idris   60%
    - Leonard   40%

- Profit share, effective from 1 January 20X3:

    - Idris   50%
    - Leonard   30%
    - Patricia   20%

- Goodwill was valued at £20000 on 31 December 20X2.

- Goodwill is to be introduced into the partners' capital accounts on 31 December and then eliminated on 1 January.

(a) Prepare the capital account for Patricia, the new partner, showing clearly the balance carried down as at 1 January 20X3.

Capital account – Patricia

	£		£

(b) Complete the following sentences by selecting the appropriate phrases from the picklists in each case:

The terms on which partners operate in business together are set out in

[   ].

Picklist:

Their partnership agreement
The Partnership Act
Their contract of employment

Where a partner is charged interest on their drawings, the amount of interest is

[   ].

Picklist:

Debited to their capital account
Debited to their current account
Credited to their capital account
Credited to their current account

Task 2.3

This task is about partnership accounts.

You have the following information about a partnership business:

- The financial year ends on 31 July.

- The partners at the beginning of the year were Grace and Harry.

- Jamal was admitted to the partnership on 1 February 20X6.

- Partners' annual salaries, effective to 31 January 20X6:

  - Grace   £15,600
  - Harry   £19,200
  - Jamal   nil

- Partners' annual salaries, effective from 1 February 20X6:

  - Grace   £13,200
  - Harry   £16,800
  - Jamal   £6,000

- Partners' interest on capital:

  - Grace   £800 per full year
  - Harry   £1,000 per full year
  - Jamal   £500 per full year

- Profit share, effective until 31 January 20X6:

  - Grace   30%
  - Harry   70%

- Profit share, effective from 1 February 20X6:

  - Grace   40%
  - Harry   50%
  - Jamal   10%

Net profit for the year ended 31 July 20X6 was £120,000. You can assume that profits accrued evenly during the year.

Prepare the appropriation account for the partnership for the year ended 31 July 20X6.

Partnership appropriation account for the year ended 31 July 20X6

	1 August X5 – 31 January X6 £	1 February X6 – 31 July X6 £	Total £
Net profit			
Salaries:			
Grace			
Harry			
Jamal			
Interest on capital:			
Grace			
Harry			
Jamal			
Profit available for distribution			

Profit share			
Grace			
Harry			
Jamal			
Total profit distributed			

....

Task 2.4

Partnership statement of financial position (balance sheet)

This task is about preparing a partnership statement of financial position.

You are preparing the statement of financial position for the Jessop Partnership for the year ended 31 October 20X7. The partners are Malcolm and Rose.

All the necessary year end adjustments have been made, except for the transfer of profit to the current accounts of the partners.

Before sharing profits the balances of the partners' current accounts are:

- Malcolm   £400 debit
- Rose   £230 credit

Each partner is entitled to £7,250 profit share.

(a) Calculate the credit balance of each partner's current account after sharing profits. Fill in the answers below.

Current account balance: Malcolm	£	
Current account balance: Rose	£	

Note: these balances will need to be transferred into the statement of financial position of the partnership which follows.

You have the following trial balance. All the necessary year-end adjustments have been made.

(b) Prepare a statement of financial position (balance sheet) for the partnership as at 31 October 20X7. You need to use the partners' current account balances that you have just calculated. Do NOT use brackets, minus signs or dashes.

Jessop Partnership
Trial balance as at 31 October 20X7

	Dr £	Cr £
Accruals		970
Allowance for receivables		1,280
Allowance for receivables adjustment	130	
Bank		2,140
Capital – Malcolm		18,000
Capital – Rose		22,000
Cash	250	
Closing inventory (stock)	9,450	9,450
Current account – Malcolm	400	
Current account – Rose		230
Depreciation expense	2,440	
Disposal of non-current (fixed) asset	2,100	
Furniture & fittings accumulated depreciation		9,240
Furniture & fittings at cost	32,980	
Marketing	17,930	
Opening inventory	21,780	
Purchases	88,810	
Payables (purchases) ledger control account		7,620
Sales		179,610
Receivables (sales) ledger control account	35,090	
Wages	41,370	
VAT		2,190
Total	252,730	252,730

Jessop Partnership
Statement of financial position (balance sheet) as at 31 October 20X7

	Cost £	Depreciation £	Carrying amount (net book value) £
Non-current (fixed) assets			
Current assets			
Current liabilities			
Net current assets			
Net assets			
Financed by:	Malcolm	Rose	Total

PRACTICE ASSESSMENT 1
ACCOUNTS PREPARATION II

ANSWERS

Section 1

Task 1.1

(a) **Receivables (sales) ledger control account**

	£		£
Balance b/d	16,360	Bank	142,650
Sales day book	150,480	Discounts allowed	8,920
		Balance c/d	15,270
	166,840		166,840

(b) **Cash in till**

	£		£
Balance b/d	300	Cash purchases	400
Cash sales	3,250	Cash banked	2,900
		Balance c/d	250
	3,550		3,550

Task 1.2

(a)

£ 3,780

(17,250 + 6,250 + 1,280 − 21,000)

(b)

Balances	Debit ✓	Credit ✓	No change ✓
Income		✓	
Trade receivables (debtors)			✓
Trade payables (creditors)	✓		
Bank		✓	
Expenses			✓

(c)

	✓
Assets + Liabilities = Capital	
Assets – Liabilities = Capital	✓
Assets = Liabilities - Capital	
Assets = Liabilities + Capital	✓

Section 2

Task 2.1

(a)

Martha Tidfill
Income statement (profit and loss account) for the year ended 31 August 20X4

	£	£
Sales		199,560
Opening inventory (stock)	17,690	
Purchases	105,280	
Closing inventory	(15,200)	
Cost of goods sold		(107,770)
Gross profit		91,790
Less:		
Depreciation expense	4,750	
Discounts allowed	1,920	
Heat and light	11,620	
Office costs	27,690	
Wages	19,990	
Total expenses		(65,970)
Net profit		25,820

(b)

	✓
Non-current (fixed) assets	
Current assets	
Current liabilities	✓
Non-current liabilities	

(c)

	✓
Relevance	
Prudence	✓
Comparability	
Ease of understanding	

Task 2.2

(a) Capital account – Patricia

	£		£
Goodwill	4,000	Balance b/d	0
Balance c/d	21,000	Bank	25,000
	25,000		25,000

(b) The terms on which partners operate in business together are set out in

their partnership agreement.

Where a partner is charged interest on their drawings, the amount of interest is

debited to their current account.

Task 2.3

Partnership appropriation account for the year ended 31 July 20X6

	1 August X5 – 31 January X6 £	1 February X6 – 31 July X6 £	Total £
Net profit	60,000	60,000	120,000
Salaries:			
Grace	7,800	6,600	14,400
Harry	9,600	8,400	18,000
Jamal	0	3,000	3,000
Interest on capital:			
Grace	400	400	800
Harry	500	500	1,000
Jamal	0	250	250
Profit available for distribution	41,700	40,850	82,550

Profit share			
Grace	12,510	16,340	28,850
Harry	29,190	20,425	49,615
Jamal		4,085	4,085
Total profit distributed	41,700	40,850	82,550

Task 2.4

Partnership statement of financial position (balance sheet)

(a)

Current account balance: Malcolm	£	6,850
Current account balance: Rose	£	7,480

(b) **Jessop Partnership**
Statement of financial position (balance sheet) as at 31 October 20X7

	Cost £	Depreciation £	Carrying amount (net book value) £
Non-current (fixed) assets	32,980	9,240	23,740
Current assets			
Inventory (stock)		9,450	
Receivables (debtors)		33,810	
Cash		250	
		43,510	
Current liabilities			
Accruals	970		
Payables (creditors)	7,620		
Bank overdraft	2,140		
VAT	2,190		
		12,920	
Net current assets			30,590
Net assets			54,330
Financed by:	**Malcolm**	**Rose**	**Total**
Capital accounts	18,000	22,000	40,000
Current accounts	6,850	7,480	14,330
			54,330

PRACTICE ASSESSMENT 2
ACCOUNTS PREPARATION II

Time allowed: 2 hours

Section 1

Task 1.1

This task is about finding missing figures in ledger accounts where the records are incomplete.

You are working on the financial statements of a business for the year ended 30 November 20X4. The business is not registered for VAT. You have the following information:

Invoices for credit purchases   £38,460
Receipts for cash purchases   £2,450

	Balance at 1 Dec 20X3	Balance at 30 Nov 20X4
Payables (creditors)	15,470	9,280
Bank overdraft	1,340	2,190

The chequebook stubs reveal that cheques for £42,770 were paid to credit suppliers. The paying in slip stubs show that cheques from credit customers of £51,890 were banked.

The owner informs you that he withdrew cash from the bank account via automated teller machines, and that some of this money he used for his own personal expenditure.

(a) Using the figures given above, prepare the bank account for the year ended 30 November 20X4. Show clearly cash drawings as the balancing figure.

Bank account

	£		£

(b) Find the figure for returns to credit suppliers by preparing the payables (purchases) ledger control account for the year ended 30 November 20X4. Use the figures given on the previous page.

Payables ledger control

	£		£

Task 1.2

This task is about calculating missing balances and the accounting equation.

You are given the following information about a shop for one financial year:

Sales were £95,200 in the year, all at a mark-up of 60%. The opening inventory (stock) was £22,560 and the closing inventory was £18,420.

(a) Calculate the purchases figure for the year.

£

(b) Identify whether each of the following balances is presented as a current asset, a current liability or neither on the face of the statement of financial position (balance sheet).

Balances	Current asset ✓	Current liability ✓	Neither ✓
Accrual			
Opening inventory (stock)			
Prepayment			
Loan from bank payable in five years			
Bank overdraft			

(c) Which of the following is best described as a current liability? Choose ONE answer.

	✓
An amount that has been received in advance from a customer	
An allowance for receivables	
Goods for resale that will be sold next month	
Cash in hand	

Section 2

Task 2.1

This task is about preparing financial statements for sole traders.

You have the following trial balance for a sole trader, Tom Kassam. All the necessary year-end adjustments have been made.

(a) Prepare an income statement (profit and loss account) for the business for the year ended 31 May 20X6.

Tom Kassam

Trial balance as at 31 May 20X6

	Dr £	Cr £
Accruals		980
Administration expenses	12,060	
Bank	1,730	
Capital		14,000
Closing inventory (stock)	14,320	14,320
Depreciation expense	3,880	
Discounts allowed	1,470	
Distribution expenses	25,340	
Drawings	17,790	
Furniture & fittings accumulated depreciation		6,480
Furniture & fittings at cost	24,800	
Opening inventory	12,830	
Prepayments	1,260	
Purchases	99,990	
Payables (purchases) ledger control account		15,940
Sales		201,560
Receivables (sales) ledger control account	18,450	
VAT		2,970
Wages	22,330	
	256,250	256,250

Tom Kassam

Income statement (profit and loss account) for the year ended 31 May 20X6

	£	£
Sales		
Cost of goods sold		
Gross profit		
Total expenses		
Net profit		

(b) Indicate where the VAT balance should be shown in the financial statements. Choose ONE from:

	✓
Non-current (fixed) assets	
Current assets	
Current liabilities	
Non-current liabilities	

(c) Which of the following amounts will appear in both the income statement (profit and loss account) and the statement of financial position (balance sheet)?

	✓
Drawings	
Capital	
Opening inventory (stock)	
Closing inventory (stock)	

Task 2.2

This task is about accounting for partnerships.

You have the following information about a partnership:

The partners are Nigel and Paula.

- Gavin was admitted to the partnership on 1 June 20X7 when he paid £18,500 into the bank account.

- Profit share, effective until 31 May 20X7:

  - Nigel   25%
  - Paula   75%

- Profit share, effective from 1 June 20X7:

  - Nigel   30%
  - Paula   50%
  - Gavin   20%

- Goodwill was valued at £50,000 on 31 May 20X7.

- Goodwill is to be introduced into the partners' capital accounts on 31 May and then eliminated on 1 June.

(a) Prepare the capital account for Gavin, the new partner, showing clearly the balance carried down as at 1 June 20X7.

Capital account – Gavin

	£		£

(b) Identify whether each of the following statements is true or false.

	True ✓	False ✓
When a partner retires from a partnership, they must always be paid what they are owed in cash.		
If the partners agree to change their profit shares, this must take effect from the beginning of the accounting period whatever the partners may agree between themselves		

Task 2.3

This task is about partnership accounts.

(a) You have the following information about a partnership:

- The financial year ends on 30 September 20X5.

- The partners are William, Richard and Steve.

- Partners' annual salaries:

    - William   £15,600
    - Richard   £17,200
    - Steve   £12,900

- Partners' capital account balances as at 30 September 20X5:

    - William   £100,000
    - Richard   £80,000
    - Steve   £60,000

Interest on capital is charged at 1% per annum on the capital account balance at the end of the financial year.

- The partners share the remaining profit of £72,000 as follows:

    - William   30%
    - Richard   45%
    - Steve   25%

- Partners' drawings for the year:

    - William   £22,890
    - Richard   £51,250
    - Steve   £17,240

Prepare the current accounts for the partners for the year ended 30 September 20X5. Show clearly the balances carried down. You MUST enter zeros where appropriate in order to obtain full marks. Do NOT use brackets, minus signs or dashes.

Current accounts

	William £	Richard £	Steve £		William £	Richard £	Steve £
Balance b/d	0	1,230	950	Balance b/d	200	0	0

Task 2.4

Partnership statement of financial position (balance sheet)

This task is about preparing a partnership statement of financial position (balance sheet).

You are preparing the statement of financial position for the Calnan Partnership for the year ended 31 March 20X2. The partners are Bernard and Jessica.

All the necessary year-end adjustments have been made, except for the transfer of profit to the current accounts of the partners.

Before sharing profits the balances of the partners' current accounts are:

- Bernard   £320 credit
- Jessica   £80 debit

Each partner is entitled to £4,230 profit share.

(a) Calculate the credit balance of each partner's current account after sharing profits. Fill in the answers below.

Current account balance: Bernard	£	
Current account balance: Jessica	£	

Note: these balances will need to be transferred into the statement of financial position of the partnership which follows.

You have the following trial balance. All the necessary year-end adjustments have been made.

(b) Prepare a statement of financial position (balance sheet) for the partnership as at 31 March 20X2. You need to use the partners' current account balances that you have just calculated. Do NOT use brackets, minus signs or dashes.

Calnan Partnership
Trial balance as at 31 March 20X2

	Dr £	Cr £
Accruals		430
Allowance for receivables		820
Allowance for receivables adjustment	155	
Bank	6,980	
Capital – Bernard		16,400
Capital – Jessica		21,200
Cash	150	
Closing inventory (stock)	8,440	8,440
Current account – Bernard		320
Current account – Jessica	80	
Depreciation expense	1,895	
Disposal of non-current (fixed) asset		300
Furniture & fittings accumulated depreciation		7,690
Furniture & fittings at cost	26,330	
Marketing	12,430	
Opening inventory	9,550	
Purchases	77,860	
Payables (purchases) ledger control account		13,440
Sales		127,490
Receivables (sales) ledger control account	28,970	
Wages	25,880	
VAT		2,190
Total	198,720	198,720

Calnan Partnership
Statement of financial position (balance sheet) as at 31 March 20X2

	Cost £	Depreciation £	Carrying amount (net book value) £
Non-current (fixed) assets			
Current assets			
Current liabilities			
Net current assets			
Net assets			
Financed by:	Bernard	Jessica	Total

PRACTICE ASSESSMENT 2
ACCOUNT PREPARATION II

ANSWERS

Section 1

Task 1.1

(a) Bank account

	£		£
Receivables (debtors)	51,890	Balance b/d	1,340
		Drawings	7,520
		Cash for purchases	2,450
Balance c/d	2,190	Payables (creditors)	42,770
	54,080		54,080

(b) Payables (purchases) ledger control

	£		£
Payments	42,770	Balance b/d	15,470
Returns (bal fig)	1,880	Invoices	38,460
Balance c/d	9,280		
	53,930		53,930

Task 1.2

(a)

£ 55,360

Workings

	£	%
Sales	95,200	160
Cost of goods sold (95200 x 100/160)	59,500	100
Gross profit	35,700	60
Opening inventory (stock)	22,560	
Purchases (bal fig)	55,360	
Closing inventory	(18,420)	
Cost of goods sold (from above)	59,500	

(b)

Balances	Current asset ✓	Current liability ✓	Neither ✓
Accrual		✓	
Opening inventory (stock)			✓
Prepayment	✓		
Loan from bank payable in five years			✓
Bank overdraft		✓	

(c)

	✓
An amount that has been received in advance from a customer	✓
An allowance for receivables	
Goods for resale that will be sold next month	
Cash in hand	

Section 2

Task 2.1

(a)

Tom Kassam
Income statement (profit and loss account) for the year ended 31 May 20X6

	£	£
Sales		201,560
Opening inventory (stock)	12,830	
Purchases	99,990	
Closing inventory	(14,320)	
Cost of goods sold		(98,500)
Gross profit		103,060
Less:		
Depreciation expense	3,880	
Discounts allowed	1,470	
Distribution expenses	25,340	
Administration expenses	12,060	
Wages	22,330	
Total expenses		(65,080)
Net profit		37,980

(b)

	✓
Non-current (fixed) assets	
Current assets	
Current liabilities	✓
Non-current liabilities	

(c)

	✓
Drawings	
Capital	
Opening inventory (stock)	
Closing inventory (stock)	✓

Task 2.2

(a) Capital account – Gavin

	£		£
Goodwill	10,000	Balance b/d	0
Balance c/d	8,500	Bank	18,500
	18,500		18,500

(b)

	True ✓	False ✓
When a partner retires from a partnership, they must always be paid what they are owed in cash.		✓
If the partners agree to change their profit shares, this must take effect from the beginning of the accounting period whatever the partners may agree between themselves		✓

Task 2.3

Current accounts

	William £	Richard £	Steve £		William £	Richard £	Steve £
Balance b/d	0	1,230	950	Balance b/d	200	0	0
Drawings	22,890	51,250	17,240	Salaries	15,600	17,200	12,900
Balance c/d	15,510	0	13,310	Interest on capital	1,000	800	600
				Profit share	21,600	32,400	18,000
				Balance c/d	0	2,080	0
	38,400	52,480	31,500		38,400	52,480	31,500

Task 2.4

Partnership statement of financial position (balance sheet)

(a)

Current account balance: Bernard	£	4,550
Current account balance: Jessica	£	4,150

(b) **Calnan Partnership**
Statement of financial position (balance sheet) as at 31 March 20X2

	Cost £	Depreciation £	Carrying amount (net book value) £
Non-current (fixed) assets	26,330	7,690	18,640
Current assets			
Inventory (stock)		8,440	
Receivables (debtors)		28,150	
Bank		6,980	
Cash		150	
		43,720	
Current liabilities			
Accruals	430		
Payables (creditors)	13,440		
VAT	2,190		
		16,060	
Net current assets			27,660
Net assets			46,300
Financed by:	**Bernard**	**Jessica**	**Total**
Capital accounts	16,400	21,200	37,600
Current accounts	4,550	4,150	8,700
			46,300

PRACTICE ASSESSMENT 3
ACCOUNTS PREPARATION II

Time allowed: 2 hours

Section 1

Task 1.1

This task is about finding missing figures in ledger accounts where the records are incomplete.

You are working on the financial statements of a business for the year ended 31 March 20X1. The business is not registered for VAT. You have the following information:

	Balance at 31 March 20X0	Balance at 31 March 20X1
Trade receivables (debtors)	39,000	27,500
Trade payables (creditors)	15,600	18,950

Discounts allowed during the year amounted to £7,400 and discounts received were £2,610. A contra entry of £830 was made between the receivables (sales) and payables (purchases) ledger control accounts.

Bank account summary

	£		£
Balance b/d	59,150	Sundry expenses	460
Trade receivables	195,150	Trade payables	84,230
Rental income	1,500	Wages	34,780
		Drawings	12,000
		Balance c/d	124,420
	255,890		255,890

(a) Calculate the figure for sales for the year by preparing the receivables (sales) ledger control account.

Receivables ledger control

	£		£

(b) Calculate the figure for purchases for the year by preparing the payables (purchases) ledger control account.

Payables ledger control

	£		£

Task 1.2

This task is about calculating missing balances and the accounting equation.

You are given the following information about a shop for one financial year:

Sales for the year amounted to £42,000, the opening inventory (stock) was £4,700 and purchases were £30,000. Gross profit margin is 33⅓%.

(a) Calculate the figure for closing inventory (stock).

£

(b) The proprietor takes goods that had cost the business £250 from the shop for her own personal consumption. Tick the boxes to show the effect of this on the accounts of the business. You must choose ONE answer for EACH line.

	Debit ✓	Credit ✓	No effect ✓
Bank			
Drawings			
Inventory (stock)			
Purchases			
Administration expenses			

(c) Which of the following statements concerning credit entries is **incorrect**? Choose ONE answer.

	✓
Credit entries record increases in capital or liabilities	
Credit entries record decreases in assets	
Credit entries record increases in profits	
Credit entries record increases in expenses	

Section 2

Task 2.1

This task is about preparing financial statements for sole traders.

You have the following trial balance for a sole trader, Colin Woodward. All the necessary year-end adjustments have been made.

(a) Prepare an income statement (profit and loss account) for the business for the year ended 31 March 20X0.

Colin Woodward
Trial balance as at 31 March 20X0

	Dr £	Cr £
Sales revenue		218,396
Purchases	81,451	
Opening inventory (stock)	11,165	
Discounts allowed	3,260	
Trade receivables (debtors) and payables (creditors)	22,863	8,367
Non-current (fixed) assets at cost	57,150	
Accumulated depreciation		24,840
Motor expenses	1,374	
Wages and salaries	84,381	
Bank balance	2,654	
Rent, rates and insurance	28,012	
General expenses	4,111	
Capital		40,891
Heat and light	12,241	
Closing inventory	13,142	13,142
Deprecation charge	8,314	
	305,636	305,636

Colin Woodward

Income statement (profit and loss account) for the year ended 31 March 20X0

	£	£
Sales		
Cost of goods sold		
Gross profit		
Total expenses		
Net profit / (loss)		

(b) Which of the following best explains the term 'current asset'?

	✓
An asset currently in use by a business	
Something a business has or uses, likely to be held for only a short time	
An amount owed to somebody else which is due for repayment soon	
Money which the business currently has in its bank account	

(c) Which of the following statements concerning journal entries is correct?

	✓
Journal entries need not be authorised	
Journal entries are used only to correct errors	
The journal is one of the ledgers of the business	
All journal entries must have a narrative explanation	

Task 2.2

This task is about accounting for partnerships.

You have the following information about a partnership:

The partners are Derek and Eva.

- Fabio was admitted to the partnership on 1 April 20X1 when he introduced £60,000 to the bank account.

- Profit share, effective until 31 March 20X1:

  - Derek   50%
  - Eva   50%

- Profit share, effective from 1 April 20X1:

  - Derek   40%
  - Eva   40%
  - Fabio   20%

- Goodwill was valued at £44,000 on 31 March 20X1.

- Goodwill is to be introduced into the partners' capital accounts on 31 March and then eliminated on 1 April.

(a) Prepare the capital account for Fabio, the new partner, showing clearly the balance carried down as at 1 April 20X1.

Capital account – Fabio

	£		£
		Balance b/d	0

(b) Complete the following sentence by selecting the appropriate phrase from the picklist in each case:

When a partner retires from a partnership business, the balance on the [   ] must be transferred to the [   ].

Picklist:

business bank account
partner's capital account
partner's current account

Task 2.3

This task is about partnership accounts. (Note for students: the two parts of this task are independent of each other, and in the assessment you would be presented with only one of them.)

(a) You have the following information about a partnership business:

- The financial year ends on 31 March.

- The partners at the beginning of the year were James, Kenzie and Lewis.

- James retired on 30 September 20X0.

- Partners' annual salaries:

  - James   £41,000
  - Kenzie   £50,000
  - Lewis   nil

- Partners' interest on capital:

  - James   £3,000 per full year
  - Kenzie   £3,000 per full year
  - Lewis   £3,000 per full year

- Profit share, effective until 30 September 20X0:

  - James   60%
  - Kenzie   20%
  - Lewis   20%

- Profit share, effective from 1 October 20X0:

  - Kenzie   75%
  - Lewis   25%

Net profit for the year ended 31 March 20X1 was £200,000. You can assume that profits accrued evenly during the year.

Prepare the appropriation account for the partnership for the year ended 31 March 20X1.

Partnership Appropriation account for the year ended 31 March 20X1

	1 April X0 – 30 September X0 £	1 October X0 – 31 March X1 £	Total £
Net profit			
Salaries:			
James			
Kenzie			
Lewis			
Interest on capital:			
James			
Kenzie			
Lewis			
Profit available for distribution			

Profit share			
James			
Kenzie			
Lewis			
Total profit distributed			

(b) You have the following information about a partnership:

- The financial year ends on 31 March.

- The partners are James, Kenzie and Lewis.

- Partners' annual salaries:

  - James   £16,500
  - Kenzie   £36,000
  - Lewis   nil

- Partners' capital account balances as at 31 March 20X1:

  - James   £50,000
  - Kenzie   £100,000
  - Lewis   £100,000

Interest on capital is charged at 6% per annum on the capital account balance at the end of the financial year.

- The partners share the remaining profit of £80,000 as follows:

  - James   30%
  - Kenzie   50%
  - Lewis   20%

- Partners' drawings for the year:

  - James   £32,000
  - Kenzie   £80,000
  - Lewis   £26,000

Prepare the current accounts for the partners for the year ended 31 March 20X1. Show clearly the balances carried down. You MUST enter zeros where appropriate in order to obtain full marks. Do NOT use brackets, minus signs or dashes.

Current accounts

	James £	Kenzie £	Lewis £		James £	Kenzie £	Lewis £
Balance b/d	800	0	0	Balance b/d	0	3,000	8,600

Task 2.4

Partnership statement of financial position (balance sheet)

This task is about preparing a partnership statement of financial position (balance sheet).

You are preparing the statement of financial position for the Jasper Partnership for the year ended 31 March 20X1. The partners are Aldo and Billy.

All the necessary year-end adjustments have been made, except for the transfer of profit to the current accounts of the partners.

Before sharing profits the balances of the partners' current accounts are:

- Aldo £366 credit
- Billy £600 credit

Each partner is entitled to £7,500 profit share.

(a) Calculate the balance of each partner's current account after sharing profits. Fill in the answers below.

Current account balance: Aldo	£	
Current account balance: Billy	£	

Note: these balances will need to be transferred into the statement of financial position of the partnership which follows.

You have the following trial balance. All the necessary year-end adjustments have been made.

(b) Prepare a statement of financial position (balance sheet) for the partnership as at 31 March 20X1. You need to use the partners' current account balances that you have just calculated. Do NOT use brackets, minus signs or dashes.

Jasper Partnership
Trial balance as at 31 March 20X1

	Dr £	Cr £
Accruals		1,190
Administration expenses	39,230	
Bank	4,276	
Capital – Aldo		35,000
Capital – Billy		20,000
Cash	690	
Closing inventory (stock)	20,570	20,570
Current account – Aldo		366
Current account – Billy		600
Depreciation charge	4,525	
Disposal of non-current (fixed) asset	750	
Motor vehicles at cost	43,500	
Motor vehicles accumulated depreciation		12,125
Opening inventory (stock)	23,027	
Allowance for receivables		830
Purchases	104,250	
Payables (purchases) ledger control account		32,950
Sales		178,785
Receivables (sales) ledger control account	53,765	
Selling expenses	12,573	
VAT		4,740
Total	307,156	307,156

Jasper Partnership
Trial balance as at 31 March 20X1

	Cost £	Depreciation £	Carrying amount (net book value) £
Non-current (fixed) assets			
Current assets			
Current liabilities			
Net current assets			
Net assets			
Financed by:	Aldo	Billy	Total

PRACTICE ASSESSMENT 3
ACCOUNT PREPARATION II

ANSWERS

Section 1

Task 1.1

(a) Receivables ledger control

	£		£
Balance b/d	39,000	Bank	195,240
Sales	191,970	Discounts allowed	7,400
		Contra with PLCA	830
		Balance c/d	27,500
	230,970		230,970

(b) Payables ledger control

	£		£
Bank	84,230	Balance b/d	15,600
Discounts received	2,610	Purchases	91,020
Contra with RLCA	830		
Balance c/d	18,950		
	106,620		106,620

Task 1.2

(a)

£ 6,700

Workings

	£	%
Sales	42,000	100
Cost of goods sold	28,000	66⅔
Gross profit	14,000	33⅓
Opening inventory (stock)	4,700	
Purchases	30,000	
Closing inventory (balancing figure)	(6,700)	
Cost of goods sold (from above)	28,000	

(b)

	Debit ✓	Credit ✓	No effect ✓
Bank			✓
Drawings	✓		
Inventory (stock)			✓
Purchases		✓	
Administration expenses			✓

(c)

	✓
Credit entries record increases in capital or liabilities	
Credit entries record decreases in assets	
Credit entries record increases in profits	
Credit entries record increases in expenses	✓

Section 2

Task 2.1

(a)

Colin Woodward
Income statement (profit and loss account) for the year ended 31 March 20X0

	£	£
Sales		218,396
Opening inventory (stock)	11,165	
Purchases	81,451	
Closing inventory	(13,142)	
Cost of goods sold		(79,474)
Gross profit		138,922
Less:		
Discounts allowed	3,260	
Motor expenses	1,374	
Heat and light	12,241	
Rent, rates and insurance	28,012	
Wages and salaries	84,381	
General expenses	4,111	
Depreciation	8,314	
Total expenses		(141,693)
Net loss		(2,771)

(b)

	✓
An asset currently in use by a business	
Something a business has or uses, likely to be held for only a short time	✓
An amount owed to somebody else which is due for repayment soon	
Money which the business currently has in its bank account	

(c)

	✓
Journal entries need not be authorised	
Journal entries are used only to correct errors	
The journal is one of the ledgers of the business	
All journal entries must have a narrative explanation	✓

Task 2.2

Capital account – Fabio

	£		£
Goodwill	8,800	Balance b/d	0
Balance c/d	51,200	Bank	60,000
	60,000		60,000

(b) When a partner retires from a partnership business, the balance on the partner's current account must be transferred to the partner's capital account.

....

Task 2.3

(a) **Partnership appropriation account for the year ended 31 March 20X1**

	1 April X0 – 30 September X0 £	1 October X0 – 31 March X1 £	Total £
Net profit	100,000	100,000	200,000
Salaries:			
James	20,500	0	20,500
Kenzie	25,000	25,000	50,000
Lewis	0	0	0
Interest on capital:			
James	1,500	0	1,500
Kenzie	1,500	1,500	3,000
Lewis	1,500	1,500	3,000
Profit available for distribution	50,000	72,000	122,000

Profit share:			
James	30,000	0	30,000
Kenzie	10,000	54,000	64,000
Lewis	10,000	18,000	28,000
Total profit distributed	50,000	72,000	122,000

(b) **Current accounts**

	James £	Kenzie £	Lewis £		James £	Kenzie £	Lewis £
Balance b/d	800	0	0	Balance b/d	0	3,000	8,600
Drawings	32,000	80,000	26,000	Salaries	16,500	36,000	0
Balance c/d	10,700	5,000	4,600	Interest on capital	3,000	6,000	6,000
				Profit share	24,000	40,000	16,000
	43,500	85,000	30,600		43,500	85,000	30,600

Task 2.4

(a) Aldo

£7,866 (366 + 7,500)

Billy

£8,100 (600 + 7,500)

(b) **Jasper Partnership**
Statement of financial position (balance sheet) as at 31 March 20X1

	Cost £	Depreciation £	Carrying amount (net book value) £
Non-current (fixed) assets			
Motor vehicles at cost	43,500	12,125	31,375
Current assets			
Inventory (stock)		20,570	
Trade receivables (53,765 – 830)		52,935	
Bank		4,276	
Cash		690	
		78,471	
Current liabilities			
Trade payables (creditors)	32,950		
VAT	4,740		
Accruals	1,190		
		38,880	
Net current assets			39,591
Net assets			70,966

Financed by:	Aldo	Billy	Total
Capital accounts	35,000	20,000	55,000
Current accounts	7,866	8,100	15,966
	42,866	28,100	70,966

Notes

Notes